KEVIN

YOUNG BLACK MALES

HAVE POTENTIAL

Contents

About the Author

Kevin Munga is a community activist who wants nothing but social change.

He is the last of three children and he is of Congolese descent, born in the northern suburbs of Paris in a small town called Sarcelles, he faced many battles in life and has had to make something from nothing. With a mother who was severely ill and a father living in another country, he did not have much guidance and that had an impact on his life.

Aged 16 Kevin realised that in the area he grew up (Croydon), it was either you became part of a local gang or you become a victim, so he believed at that specific time that adhering to a gang was the right choice, although prior to that it was never his intention.

The transition point was when he found Christ aged 19. This positive force helped him turn his life around and he is now a role model in his borough. He is currently a youth mentor, a community activist and he is in his last year of a law degree Kevin says, "I'm trying to challenge the ideology that in order to be a somebody where I am from you need road status and that the only way young black males make it where I am from is if they know how to kick a ball or write lyrics'. He has taken many different assemblies in various schools in Croydon, spoken to groups and now he works with Inspirational Youth with the aim to continue sharing the learning from his experiences. He is a public speaker he has spoken at venues in London and now he wants to speak internationally. He wants other young men to find their own mission in life.

Kevin has a dream and he will not stop until it happens.

Overview of slavery

Let me highlight the pain our people went through, and allow you as readers to imagine the depths of pain in which we endured. 1619 our people also known as African slaves were brought from Jamestown, Virginia. Our ancestors were enslaved due to the demand for many labourers for the sugar, tobacco and cotton plantations. As paid labourers were too expensive, and the indigenous people had largely been wiped out by disease and conflict. The oppressors of our people turned to Africa to provide cheap labour in the form of slaves, to elaborate further, the reasons our people were enslaved was due to African political leaders who were willing to trade Human bodies for European raw materials, specifically guns that would give the powerful African's more power.

I prefer liberty with danger than peace with slavery – Jean Jacques Rousseau.[1]

---

[1] Jean-Jacques Rousseau. 2017. Quotable Quote. [ONLINE] Available at:
https://www.goodreads.com/quotes/74073-i-prefer-liberty-with-danger-than-peace-with-slavery.
[Accessed 28 September 2017].

Chapter One Gangsterism

The definition of gangsterism is subscribing to a course of action resembling organised crime. This also involves acting or conducting business in a way that is violent and totally without conscience. The use of tactics associated with gangsters includes intimidation or violence in order to achieve their main operative.

The word gangster has a different connotation to me. Personally, a gangster to me is an individual, which belongs to a gang for the following reasons; acquiring power, money, popularity, respect and attracting women. However, before I go into detail I would like to permit you to understand where and how gangsterism came about.

Did gangsterism become the escape route for young black males? A way out and did it add self-value to an individual. The first gangs emerged in America in 1920; gangsters thrived off the fear that was usually caused by their own criminal activities. In addition to this, they usually kept to themselves, operated in secret, and ensured that they protected themselves. Al Capone aka Scarface was perhaps the most notorious gangster in history. His parents were Italian immigrants; he grew up in Chicago and became a major gang leader.

How does that relate to a young black man's decision in becoming a gangster? Well Capone's crime gang ranked in as much 100 million dollars annually, many black men's parents in America, were immigrants and born in poverty, a bit like Al Capone by making so much annually he convinced people it could be done. The ideology that "crime pays" has been passed on to the younger generation and now the average black man born in poverty, also feels his only way out of poverty, is by taking part in criminal activities. Why do I say average? Because coming from an area known for welfare it takes an individual with more than the average mind to surpass the urge of becoming dishonest to society. This idea can often be perceived as a curse and I believe as black males we need to challenge the idea that "crime pays".

Psychologically once something is proven to be done, another human being will also believe they will be able to do it but if crime pays, why is there always a sad ending? In addition, why it is only temporary?

Surely, there is another way in which one can acquire financial gain and live happily ever after. The energy that is used to sell drugs or get involved in criminality is the same energy that can be used to acquire financial gain legitimately. However, is it all about the money? What about respect? Take Bumpy Johnson, born Ellsworth Raymond Johnson a Mob Boss and drug trafficker. He was considered as a hero in the eyes of many who lived in Harlem where he resided. Due to the fact, they were impressed a black man could cut deals with the Italian Mafia.

Leroy Nicolas Barnes was known as Mr. Untouchable, for one to be called such a name surely he was respected. He was also a drug lord and crime boss. Then you take Frank Lucas he was a gangster and kingpin and many wannabe gangsters in today's society look up to

Him, some have even renamed themselves, Frank Lucas. He is a good example as he grew up in North Carolina in the 1930's; many American's in the rural south were poor at this time.

Most African- American suffered the deepest poverty. As the oldest boy, he had to find a way to survive; he wanted survival for the family so turning to crime he believed was the right decision. It just shows that the average man succumbs under pressure and that was the way HE CHOSE to handle it. He began as a thief and was doing minor crimes. In his late teens, he got a job as a truck driver for a pipe company; you would think that would be the deliverance for his family and a stable income. However, he was caught in the act of sleeping with the manager's daughter. Which resulted in him fighting his manager and he also stole money from the company. In addition to this, he set the establishment on fire. His mother pleaded with him to move to New York to prevent his arrest. Arriving there, people advised him to get a job and earn money the legitimate way, but he failed to see the bigger picture.

He saw how real money was being made through illegal practices such as drugs and unauthorized gambling. In addition, I quote "the average man adheres to what's glorified and glamorized around him". He was robbing at gunpoint and getting involved in criminal activities. When does the respect come in? Alternatively, a sentence usually used in the streets of London earning stripes. Frank Lucas's efforts were not unnoticed, Bumpy Johnson the long-time Harlem gangster, who controlled gambling and extortion operations had noticed him and became close friends with Lucas. Here is what many people on the street will consider as respect, but initially does that respect last? After Frank Lucas was arrested eventually he became an informant to police and there is a consensus that one of his

Calibre should never cooperate with police, ultimately this would mean he breached the code, this would also mean he lost his street credibility, once again the respect he once looked for was nothing but temporary.

How has gangsterism evolved since the retirement or death of these notorious black gangsters and drug traffickers, who were active as early as 1932, in all the different types of crimes they were involved in?

How does crime look in the more recent years? In 2002, a film entitled paid in full spoke about the rise of three friends, who became top earners through drug deals. The person that was portrayed as the main character in the film was not always a bad person he dropped out of school early, from as early as the 9th grade, and worked in local dry cleaners. The man I am speaking of is Azie Faison who by the age of 21 started earning between $90,000-$100-00 a week. However, there is a reason behind it; Faison maintains that the film Scarface strongly influenced his decision to become a drug dealer. Funny enough for me the movie paid in full made me want to become a drug dealer myself, this just goes to show that what we watch and listen to has a major impact on us.

The wakeup call for Faison was when someone attempted to take his life and he was shot nine times. After that, he departed from drug dealing and adopted the mission to keep young people from the path he once chose.

He was highly disappointed in the production in the film, which portrayed him, as I believe it glorified drug deals and the lifestyle instead of condemning it. I feel like the movie did not show the terrible side effects of how dangerous it is to be a drug dealer. In

Addition, I feel the film may have influenced many in the decision to become drug dealers.

In like manner, America was also known for criminal street gang's drive-by shootings, homicides and brutal home invasion as well as many accounts of robbery. Similar to this, the department of justice states they are approximately 175,000 to 200,000 gang members in the district of California.

As previously, stated gangsterism is defined by subscribing to a course of action resembling organized crime. In conjunction with this, a gang member by definition is "any person who actively participates in any gang with knowledge that its members engage in or have engaged in a pattern of criminal gang activity, it is also who will promote or assist any felonious criminal activity conducted by the gang itself.

Let's look at some of the facts. From 1955 to 1965, the African American gangs increased, with more members joining especially in central Los Angeles and Compton. The cause of that was unity amongst African Americans, these young black males wanted protection so they decided to form groups. In the late 1960's the two most violent gangs emerged known as the Crips and bloods. Both gangs known for their distinctive colours, the Crips were represented with the colour blue and as for the bloods, it was red. Likewise, the year 1970 was when both Crips and bloods divided into smaller groups, smaller gangs or smaller sets. Both gangs started to claim certain territories belonged to them. The painful (hurtful) fact is that some of the gang members were as young as the age of 14 years old. How did the youngsters prove they were worthy of being in the gang?

They were sometimes initiated by fighting people who already belonged to the gang. Alternatively, they needed to commit a crime in the neighbourhood I do not believe by them committing a crime as such, they were ready for the streets I just believe they did so in order to fit in and unfortunately, they believed that to be a somebody, to gain street credibility or any type of respect the only way was through criminality. In order for gangs at the time to be unique, they would establish trademarks such as colours, hand signs sometimes numbers to represent the area code.

However, how does that relate to a young black's decision in wanting to become a gang member in London? America's a force and has a major impact on the world especially England, but to be precise I will highlight the impact they have on London. In South London, there was also Crips and Bloods in the borough of Lambeth the impact meant we had young black males representing the colour Red and blue. The rivalry between the two became one of the bloodiest in the recent years and a few had unfortunately lost their lives.

When speaking of a gang member or drug dealers they are just different forms of "gangsterism". The reasons are always the same being wrongly influenced; "nothing but gangsters as role models in the area" so the younger generation does not know any better. Being born in a state of poverty is always a major one too and not having any hope that things will get better. Having a darker skin colour than your peers often, plays on a black young person's mind, you subconsciously think they have a better chance of acquiring wealth or becoming someone great in the future because they are not restricted by their race and you are. Respect? You believe the only way to get respect is on the streets because you don't see many black men excelling in your area unless it's through sports or music,

Knowing you may not be an athlete or lyrically gifted. You develop the urge of wanting to also live a purposeful life and have a name and sometimes young black males believe their only shot is acquiring street fame.

It is something that has been passed on to us by the older generation, is it a cycle but as we know every cycle can be broken, we can take the decision today and break this cycle prove the government wrong and achieve our dreams because anything is possible.

Chapter Two Black on Black crime

What comes to mind when you hear black on black crime?

It is normally the act of one black man inflicting harm on another black man. However, I believe it is deeper than that when we speak on the sensitive topic of black on black crime we see hatred, envy, revenge and sometimes respect. Why does respect also fall in the bracket? Some of the black on black crimes that are committed by gang members derive from rivalry and for one to gain the respect they attack their fellow brother.

They are stereotypes and other things, which contribute in the misconception of us being considered as the lowest race, we do not make matters any better by killing each other. Despite the fact that white police officers in America kill blacks, there is a far larger amount of black bodies being sent to the morgues by black killers.

Through my research, I discovered that a hustler named "Fast Willie" explained why he robbed and beat up black people that are supposed to be his brothers. His response was he commits crimes against the African Americans because that is whom he lives amongst, and that's what police will let him get away with. This statement is from the 1970's he also states that would be impossible for him to commit crimes in Deerfield which is a north Chicago neighbourhood that's predominantly white and 96% white today. At that time, the state officials and criminal system were known for

Punishing black criminals more harshly when their victims were white as oppose to when the victims were black.

However, is that enough of a reason for black on black crime?

Certain things contribute for blacks to be more inclined to a life of crime and brutality to their fellow brothers. Among white and black families with similar incomes, white families are much more likely to live in a good neighbourhood with high-quality schools, day-care options, parks, playgrounds and many different transportation options.

I believe that integration that disregards both class and race would be the answer; it would create more multicultural communities resulting in fewer crimes being committed.

Similarly, the black lives matter was a movement created in order to raise awareness, it is blatant you can get it from the title "Black Lives Matter". Two-thousand and twelve was the birth of black lives matter after, the defendant i.e. murderer of victim Trayvon Martin was found not guilty of the crimes he committed. Mr. George Zimmerman was acquitted and did not go into incarceration for the murder of 17-year old Martin. This issue will be spoken about further in my next chapter. The other contributors to black on black crime are things like music, which have a major impact on the young teens in this generation. They are stories of the defendants confirming that it was the music they listened to that made them kill or attempt to kill someone, and when you dig deeper it is black males killing each other. Black males trying to copy what their favourite rappers say in their lyrics. I am not saying it is wrong to rap about the life you once lived or your realities but it is also your duty to ensure that

Other young black males do not go down a route of crime that is influenced by YOUR message.

I believe in transparency but I am against the glorification of crime. As stated by Ibn Ali please take care of your own people, no one will take care of us except us these young men are our responsibility and we should not put that burden on anybody else. Ibn Ali is a man who went viral after breaking up a fight between two young black males who were about to fight in the street, those young men were wrongly advised and urged by the crowd to fight, the crowd was even filming the altercation. However, when Ali stepped in he stopped the fight and spoke wisely to the pair that was fighting and declared that they should end it. Ali is an example and we need more people to take responsibility for our young men.

The last thing that contributes to black on black crime is the jail sentences, you have young black males who have no fear to afflict such harm on another because they are more inclined to get a lighter sentence in the UK as oppose to America. In America, a criminal can serve up to a hundred years behind bars, meaning they will not see daylight again, and in some states, people get the death penalty, the fear of having daylight prohibited forever is also a method for crime prevention. But by giving someone just an insignificant punishment for the murder, they have committed, that is just a push and encouragement for other teenagers to think it is acceptable to kill each other knowing the punishment will not be severe, in my opinion.

Don't get me wrong I am not speaking for the people who are wrongly accused and those that had the misfortune of being misrepresented or judged in an unfair way. I am speaking about the

Killers who have no remorse for the crime they have committed. I believe a punishment is installed to correct an individual and if a person has no remorse for the crime committed. Their punishment should be a message unto others and fear that they may also receive this punishment if they decide to commit the same crime, a crime, which prevents a mother from seeing her son again; a crime, which erases and ends an entire generation the crime of murder is to be taken extremely seriously.

Chapter Three Injustice & Police Brutality

The word injustice is described as the violation of the rights of others, unjust or unfair action or treatment.

The chapter of injustice and Police brutality highlights some of the things that I consider unjust thanks to movements like Black Lives Matter which started to broadcast the ways in which black people are left powerless at the hands of the state.

The US police killed at least 258 black people in 2016, thirty nine of these people were unarmed, four were killed by police stun guns and another nine died in custody. Although some of the killings were in jail the majority of these killings were black people that were fatally shot.

So how does injustice and police brutality link?

Brutality looks the same as it did in the 1960's the harsh treatment towards African Americans from government officials was not uncommon and it is not uncommon now. This raises the question "Are the blacks in America or across the world really free?

Michael Jordan spoke out and said;

"I was raised by parents who taught me to love people regardless of their race or background, so I am saddened and frustrated by the

Divisive rhetoric and racial tensions that seem to be getting worse as of late. I know this country is better than that, he concluded by saying I can no longer stay silent. We need to find solutions that ensure people of colour receive fair and equal treatment. [2]

Alton Sterling's killing on the 5th of July 2016 was the last straw for members of the public to go crazy. He was the 184th black person to be killed in 2016. Thousands of protestors gathered outside the store where Alton Sterling was dead, demanding justice. Sterling was shot because allegedly they believed he had a gun; however, he was legally authorised to carry it. It can be argued that his skin colour contributed in him being shot, is it a crime to be black and legally carry a gun? This is where my frustration stems from. The colour of your skin should not make you more vulnerable and you should never be perceived as more dangerous than someone else because of your race.

Bringing it closer to home the death of Mark Duggan in the UK, in North London Tottenham. Members of the public and his family did not take his death lightly either; this resulted in the worst riots in England's recent history.

For me, the reason behind the riots was more than Mark Duggan it was the people vs. the authorities. Many who engaged in the riots felt they were poor; many went to get things they could not afford whilst the others went to make money, the remaining were raging against the machine we call society.

---

[2] Michael Jordan. 2016. Michael Jordan breaks is silence on social issues. [ONLINE] Available at: http://edition.cnn.com/2016/07/25/sport/michael-jordan-comments-race-police/index.html. [Accessed 28 September 2017].

Serious violence took place all over London especially in Croydon; burning buildings, well-known businesses destroyed such as Reeve's furniture store. Where I am from teenagers have had hatred against the police, so the shooting of Mark Duggan could only make matters worse. The battle became us against them when I say us it does not mean I was involved it just indicates that the police labelled anyone who took part as a criminal.

Whereas I see those people that had a part to play as my family and part of the community. Many people who got involved in the looting were not criminals they just joined everyone as it was what was happening at the time.

The last incident I would like to mention happened in Paris, something very unjustifiable. This took place earlier in 2017, the articles online read a young black man was in hospital after he was "raped with a police truncheon". In other words, a police baton, this once again created riots and protests; the riots took place in a Northern suburb of Paris, and the reason why the topic is heart-breaking is that I was born in a northern suburb of Paris myself. I know what it is like growing up as a young black male in the suburbs of Paris it is not easy.

Until this day, there was no valuable reason as to why he was raped. The fact that the police officers in France who raped him were not incarcerated is proof that there is no justice and that the system is beyond corrupt. Regardless of anything that Theo may have done, how is raping him justifiable in any way, shape, or form? What type of correction is rape?

Moreover, there is a consensus that rape in slavery meant "Soul murder", some of the victims of rape in slavery suffered from

Depression and this resulted in them having anger and low self-esteem. Therefore, my question is what was the aim of those police officers who afflicted such harm on Theo. In an emotional video, the 22-year-old said his wounds have not yet recovered but despite that, he still told everyone to remain calm. Despite the fact that Theo wanted peace, the riots in

Paris frantically spread across the country. The violent police assault on Theo is yet another example of systematic police brutality and it is serious, incidents like this should never happen again. Police are public servants they should be there for us not against us.

"The white robe has been exchanged by a police uniform" – Malcolm X

The banners read justice for Theo, AGREED justice for Theo and any other young man who has been a victim of police brutality.

Chapter Four Stereotypes

The average black man is often stereotyped after slavery ended the intellectual capacity of black people was regularly questioned, this may have suggested that black people were considered to be under-achievers, the media contributed in making us look less intelligent than we are in 1985 stated Jesse Jackson.

However, what are the modern stereotypes in the recent years? The stereotypes are, as followed blacks are perceived as absent fathers, gang members or serving time in jail. This is often the stereotypes given to the average black man. Growing up I did feel judgement and I did feel like I need to work twice as hard as anyone from another race. Every stop and search that I ever encountered I felt targeted or under pressure. However, at the age of 21, I got the epiphany that my race, the stereotypes or the fact that I have to work twice as hard does not matter. I realised that nothing good in life comes easy and that working hard should not be a problem. I also understood that there is no limitation apart from the ones I create.

There is a consensus that is built around black males for their tremendous ability in sport and their lyrical talent. However, I personally believe black men are not always advised to go into further education and become professionals. It seems as if society only focuses on congratulating black men when they are rappers or athletes but rarely for their academics.

In France, the ethnic minority is encouraged from the age of 16 to do things that are more practical and they are often told that they will be better with their hands; they are advised to be plumbers or electricians. For some reason, they do not tell them to go into higher education despite the fact that the students may be excelling in school. Of course, there are always expectations and I am sure some French teachers do encourage higher education for the ethnic minority, but the majority of students are not encouraged enough. My view on this issue is that regardless of not being encouraged enough we should still seek education regardless of whosoever doubts that we can become professionals, we shall BECOME. It is still our duty to attempt. I rejoice in the fact that we have the ability to be great in sports or in music. However, I believe we need heroes in every sector.

J-Cole a famous rapper says in one of his songs "what's the price for a black man's life? I check the toe tag, not one zero insight I turn the TV on not one hero insight unless he dribbles or he fiddles with mics" this lyric reiterates my point.

Despite the fact that we excel in sports and music I believe our voices are mandatory in decision-making, and I believe nothing stops us from becoming renowned as professionals.

Back to my other points as I previously stated the average black man is often wrongly stereotyped as the absent black father. The scandal of the absent black fathers in the UK research shows that black teenagers have actually stated, having a weapon is an essential accessory. Similarly, a handbag is to a woman. The question as to why there is crime amongst the black community keeps rising, the

Answer is that the male adult in the house has gone and this happens to be the father. It is having a devastating effect on young black males and unfortunately, it encourages them to turn to drugs, gangs, the streets and crime in general.

Regardless of these facts I still stand that coming from an area known for welfare does not give an excuse for us to result to violence and that the myth of the absent father should only be motivation for us to excel. It should be a push for us to be nothing like the fathers that left the household; it should be motivation for us to be an example to our kids or future kids.

Young black men killing each other, facing a sentence and joining a gang has become the norm. I call for a revolution and state that seeing black professionals should become the new common consensus, without the phrase "he is trying to defy the odds".

Only one in sixteen black men are in senior management roles and only one in thirteen are in any managing position. The statistics speak and the numbers need to change. If we are not given enough opportunities we need to create them we need to stick together as one and help one another for our own benefit, this will also benefit society as a whole and equip us in moving forward.

Chapter Five Masculinity

Society often has a distorted idea of what it means to be a man. According to Doug Wilson, masculinity is one who takes responsibility. The Christian faith states anyone who evades responsibility i.e. who does not attempt providing for his family would not be considered a proper man. That is from a point of view based on my faith. However, after I entirely describe how a man should be in my opinion. I will elaborate on what I believe SOCIETY's idea is of how a man should be.

My definition is of one that realises all of his decisions have a strong possibility of affecting the people he loves. I believe that a real man tries his best to make sure his decisions affect the people around him in a good way, a real man shows emotion if he needs to and a real man does not have to prove anything, he is free from people's opinions and has a mind completely of his own.

What does it mean to be a man currently in society; many men in this generation have heard the phrase "man up".

We are taught to be tough from an early age and that is usually translated in the ability to be violent. A man in today's society is not allowed to show emotion let alone shed a tear regardless of what happens.

Even if you lost someone, close to you or overcame an obstacle?

When you want to rejoice and you happen to shed a tear, does it make you less of a man? Or more a man because you can express your feelings freely and victoriously? What does being a man entail?

Do you have to keep your emotions locked in; it is almost as if being a man requires you to wear a mask. It seems as if it requires you to keep on this façade. However, whether we may realise it or not, this mentality does more damage to humanity than most of us actually realise. We have created an image that prevents men from being true to them.

To elaborate on this point, we associate the word male with "dominance". Most men refuse to talk about their emotions they hold it in and ultimately this turns into a seed that is translated into pain and sorrow, which eventually leads to depression.

This also influences some of the decisions young black males make. The average black male adopts this ideology and takes certain decisions based on the image he wishes to portray but unfortunately, this image is often translated in the wrong way. This image can often become violence, street credibility, and respect. This image is sometimes protected even if it means ending up in jail or dying, this is why the misconception that has been created of what it means to be a male growing up in a deprived area needs to be eradicated.

It is impossible to address black masculinity without addressing the stereotypes that contribute to the portrayals of blacks in society. It is vital for black men to create their own perception of black masculinity in order to stop being misunderstood or mislead.

Chapter Six Black Hip Hop

I would like to give a brief history of Hip Hop in order to enable the reader to get a greater understanding of the rap culture. I want to differentiate pros and Cons of Hip Hop History and would like to elaborate on its positive contribution but how it can also have a devastating effect on young men if not used as a tool to empower the up and coming generation, UK rap has also heavily been influenced by US hip-hop

Before I go into detail about whether hip-hop adds to negative perspectives towards women or encourages violent behaviour among males, it is firstly important to understand the history of where hip-hop initially originated from and what Hip-Hop as a whole means. Rose, T (2008) defines Hip Hop as a regional motivated explosion, which mainly dwells on rebuilding communities. Rose, T (2008) also states that hip-hop is a style of well-known music originating from US black and Hispanic background. This music consists of rap as well as electronic backing.

It was first created during the early years of 1970 and was usually practiced by those that were of African American culture. Likewise, this genre of music began to get popular beyond the African American ethnic group and developed a high expansion on extremely well known social media platforms. These platforms differed from YouTube to World star hip-hop among many other hip-hop's a mixture of talents it is the art of MCing, breakdancing as well as rap.

I believe hip-hop enables one to express about almost anything. Vibe, (1999) exclaims that there were many difficulties along the way to Hip Hop becoming what it is today. However, despite the hardships, he declared that the historical knowledge of what you could learn from it now would have the potential to assist almost anyone in the game now. Moreover, there is a consensus that although Hip Hop is a powerful force, it does not make use of its position and recognition that it upholds within the music industry. The Hip Hop generation needs to have more togetherness in order to make a statement, ultimately allowing the positive side of the Hip Hop generation to defeat those that are trying to create a negative impact.

To give you a deeper understanding of the history of Hip Hop it is imperative that we are educated on the first Hip Hop song that was ever to be made. Light (1999)[3] suggests that on October 1979, a brand new music label that goes by the name of sugar hill released their first ever single called "rappers delight". A few weeks later, it was to their surprise as well as to the shock of others within the community that they became Billboard's top 40 where it remained stagnant for the duration of two weeks. Likewise, this was viewed as a fulcrum as this was the first ever time that a national audience actually took notice of the genre of Hip-Hop music, and for many "rappers delight" was perceived as the end of Hip Hops beginning.

Twenty years onwards despite every set back, restriction, or failure that Hip Hop may have faced, the artists, fashion icons and actors such as Lauren Hill, Q-Tip as well as will smith all managed to make it to the top grabbing hold of the public's attention for all their mind-blowing talents.

On the contrary, since the creation of "rappers delight", Hip Hop has never really recovered from its achievement. Nevertheless, due to this record label only being formed with the intention of wanting to solely reap record sales then came the loss of what Light (1999) described as a genuine community spirit.

Moving on to the emergence of rap and how it was established. Rap is the lyrical supplement to hip-hop culture with the involvement of lyrical or poetic expressions. They are seven elements to Hip-Hop these elements are known as Saturation, language, imagery, texture, meaning, structure and flow stated by Pate (2009). These elements act as a guideline in order to assist and help in increasing x one's skills; it also helps to promote the effectiveness of your composition and improves the quality of an individual's skills. Rap caught the attention of America as this was new, it was very entertaining and it came when they least expected it. This occurred right at the establishment of disco`s decorous salon society which meant that the vast majority of America felt liberated and victorious.

The first Hip-Hop rap DJ recognized as "DJ Kool Herc". Dj Kool Herc was one of the first to create funky, well-synced compositions within his Bronx community. Nevertheless, although he wasn`t perceived as one of the most musically gifted he was still renowned as one of the most exciting and knew exactly how to catch the ears of his audiences extremely well. Likewise, Herc`s popularity came from his ability to cut and mix specific styles of music. The main specialties lied in the cultures of Jamaican dancehall music where he was always drawn in by street parties after hearing it play. With this came his contribution in the community where he would often associate himself in street activities such as riding dirt bikes, flying kites as well as playing marbles.

34

He was later on described by Vibe as a talent scout and had a top skill when it came to finding talent at his parties. However, Herc managed to maintain his spot in royalty within the empire of Hip Hop nation his reputational career decided to go down when he later was discovered selling class a drugs and because of this was sentenced to many years in prison. After he served his time, he was then able to rebuild his reputation and make a second reappearance onto the scene of Hip Hop. Throughout his time of living clean brought him many advantages, which greatly assisted him with the expansion of his success and lifelong legacies. This involved the privilege to work with many admirable

What are the advantages and disadvantages of Hip Hop?

There are many advantages. One of the many pros of Hip Hop, Hip Hop transforms learning atmospheres into exciting communities of worth and therapy where students develop, learn, and ultimately become their best. This is beneficial as it promotes general positivity and advocates on their behalf to ensure that they become best versions of themselves. Hip Hop music works perfectly great for cardiovascular exercises encourages and is good for motivation. This genre of music is a high-energy method for young people to blow off steam and assist in reinstating their mental well-being in some cases but I also believe that it depends on the lyrical content.

Hip Hop is a way of lyrical expression used so that others can release their deepest inner pains and emotion. It is an element used to permit others to comprehend the English language further and is simply a platform for them to create their own words. The lyrics from some of the songs written today assist incredibly with supporting a young person in their decision making, reason why I believe it is vital to send out a positive message. Rap music can be beneficial but it

35

Can also be used as a token to help develop the skills for teenagers that aspire to become musicians as they can be inspired through the accomplishments of artists. Hip- Hop not only helps with their rhythmic efficiency but this also supports them whilst attempting to flow well and on a beat. The therapeutic use of rap helps in combating depression ultimately causes individuals to feel a sense of mental freedom. This takes place whilst imagining you are as famous as one of your favourite Hip Hop artists and visualizing yourself at a similar place Hadley and Yancy, (2011)

This process is done in order to get you from a negative to positive. Despite the fact that Hip Hop clearly has its advantages like any other genre of music there are also disadvantages. The current years, Hip Hop has drifted towards the behaviours of aggression and violence ultimately having effects on individuals who were listening to it. Some of the content of certain lyrics found in the music has been impacting and reshaping the attitudes of our young people negatively. Today and the ideology that the violent lyrics are only there for the purpose of entertainment should be abolished I believe in entertainment and in telling your story. However, I believe that there is always a positive in a negative, the end message should not be to encourage the violence, the drugs and the nights spent behind bars. The end message should be that no matter what situation you find yourself in you can conquer it and you can turn that negative into a positive.

Perry, (2004) believes that a negative element of Hip-Hop is that it promotes racism and degrades black people. As the majority of the music incorporates the word "nigga", something that I believe can only be corrected by the musicians themselves. Hodge, (2010) emphasizes that an additional con to Hip Hop is that the young

People of today view it at as a God and choose to use it as a guideline to negatively help them to get through life. It can cause an individual to have detrimental effects, which can have a major impact on their emotional wellbeing as well as their mood. Hip Hop has the ability to enhance your brain activity and as a result, could permit you to become angry extremely quickly but with the right message, it could inspire you and make you believe in yourself so the result depends on the content.

Throughout this chapter, we have learned the importance of Hip Hop and how it positively and negatively affects the lives of young people. Similar to this we brought it back to the very first individuals that assisted in shaping the Hip Hop culture to what it currently is now. I was also able to provide you with the detail of some of the first artists in the early years of 1970 and enlightened you on how that developed Hip Hop into its current successful state now. Overall I have learned a great deal about hip-hop and been awakened about the power it holds in many different countries today. After my research, I understand about its influence I have perceived the variety of ways it can be used and demonstrated onto others its influence.

I believe Hip-Hop can be used both for positive or negative and the decision stands with us. We say we want change but do we really mean it? Is change our priority do we want fewer shootings, fewer young men dropping out of school and fewer kids being lied to that selling drugs is the way? Hip-hop is a powerful influential tool let us use it to educate the generations to come. Some artists have millions of followers; millions of kids who idolise them respect them and who are influenced by them. They are in a position of leadership so

Initially; they have the power to build or destroy it all. It ultimately comes down to the choice we make let us make the right one.

Chapter Seven Breaking barriers

(Motivational Chapter)

Breaking barriers are what every black male should do. It is often something that society disallows us from achieving which is why I cannot stress the importance of breaking barriers. Why is it that we have to over congratulate a black brother's success when he achieves something, is it based on the rarity of the achievement or is it down to the common consensus that society holds. Could it be because we can identify the struggles and recognise the work ethic and what it takes one to achieve this or is it solely approached from a non-coloured perspective with the great intent to see the individual win?

These are the many questions that occur in my head in relation to this but it is safe to say that only two out of the three that was asked remain relevant. The truth is when you're a black male yourself you are therefore able to recognise the struggles to achieve victory in one's success which ultimately gives you the go-ahead to over compliment a black male on theirs. Likewise, although this behaviour usually comes from a good heart this mentality stems from the societal agreement that "successes in black males are rare".

Now as much as we have come to terms with this unfortunate truth we still have to salute the black males that have accomplished a lot in life and have reached their fullest potential. By doing this they have defied the odds of society and have broken down one of the

Biggest barriers in history, not only have they proven to themselves that it is possible but they stand here today as history makers, legacy leavers, and world changers. Breaking the barrier as a black man is extremely important as it means it enhances the possibility for another. It is a model of hope for someone else that believes that it is impossible, and it is a statement to all the opposition that believed, success is unachievable.

One of the many black males that were able to break barriers by achieving success was Aliaume Damala Badara also known as Akon. His success first occurred within his early years as a musician. His success was identified, with his indescribable deeds and what he accomplished in Africa. Aliaume Damala also ended unemployment for over 5,000 young people, as he required them to maintain and install all the solar equipment. With the assistance of all his employees, he was able to provide solar energy in 14 different countries that were in need of electricity. Now if that is not the true definition of a black man breaking the barrier I do not know what is. Like many others, he could have remained content, but he chose to defy the odds and impact the lives of others forever.

I do not know what your dream is, what ambition you have or what goal you would like to achieve but I just want to encourage you in letting you know that it is possible. It is possible to supersede the labels that others have put on you, it is possible to rise above what your maths or science teacher has said about you, and it is possible to create change and make history. Moreover, if you ever feel in doubt just remember the name's.

Martin Luther King Jr - American Baptist minister, activist, humanitarian, and leader in the African-American Civil Rights Movement.

Nelson Mandela - South African anti-apartheid revolutionary, politician, and philanthropist, who served as President of South Africa from 1994 to 1999

Malcolm x - American Muslim minister and human rights activist.

Michael Jackson- American singer, dancer, and songwriter The King of Pop

Bob Marley- Jamaican reggae singer, songwriter, musician, and guitarist

Tupac Shakur - American rapper and actor

Barack Obama - the 44th president of the United States of America, the first African-American to be elected President of the United States

Chapter Eight Reprogramming Your Mind

The three C's that can prevent you from growing, being complacent, content and comfortable.

They are signs, which may indicate that one has become complacent, the fact that you have no fear may indicate that you are becoming complacent and I do not want this to be taken the wrong way. However, I believe that one needs the fear of God in order to have the right principals, morals, and values. The fact that you also have no fear indicates you are not taking enough risks. When there are not enough challenges in one's life that can also be taken to be complacent. There are no too small or big challenges; someone completing a degree can be a challenge whereas to someone else it can be reading an entire book.

When you fall into a routine, you need to re-evaluate your life and go back to make the improvements that are needed. The reason why routines are dangerous because they bring stagnancy when people feel complacent they often do not try to climb out of the situation they have found themselves in.

Before speaking about being content and comfortable, I would like to highlight why it is a necessity for us to revaluate our lives in order for us to grow.

When speaking of drug dealers and gang members as I have been doing throughout this book you come to the realization that there is no end goal. All there is a place of financial comfort or temporary respect. There is no way on earth that by living a dishonest life an individual can leave behind him empowerment and a righteous legacy.

The men that empowered and became world-changers had to eventually become men of integrity. We see it all the time with bandits who become rappers, politician's athletes and more. It requires growth and the need to REPROGRAM YOUR MIND. Many who left the life of crime behind such as Malcolm x had to reprogram their mind, it enabled their transition. The fact that we do not know our death dates should be enough motivation for us to be adequate and full of integrity. We have the power to bless the generations to come.

There is incredible power in contentment it but can also be dangerous when you get comfortable and you do not see the need to grow. Being content in the greater scheme of things is not a bad thing, but when one attaches it to comfort and does not see the need to grow that then turns into the inadequacy, often people can give up on life. But I am here to confirm that your heartbeat is an indication that it is not over; you have not completed everything that God has sent you on this earth to complete. Be efficient and fulfil your purpose on this earth.

Chapter Nine My Thoughts (Quotes)

"-The average man adheres to what is glorified and glamorized around him"

"-Repetition + Execution = Resilience"

"Plans + Dreams = Ambition"

"Ambition with no resilience = nothing"

"-It takes bad character from the other party to break a genuine person, don't associate with those that make you question why you are clean hearted, patient & kind"

"-Society has weird misconceptions that being more than average is solely measured on your finances. However, knowing why you are alive, discovering your talents utilising them is being more than average."

"-Trying to challenge the ideology that in order to be a somebody where I am from you need road status. And that the only way young black males make it where I am from is if they know how to kick a ball or write lyrics."

"-From the outside world, you will always appear as the individual that you're not but with that being said don't be disheartened as it does not make you look bad, but this is only a reflection of the oppressor's views of themselves."

"-Young black men killing each other facing a sentence and joining a gang has become the norm. I call for a revolution and state that seeing black professionals should become the new common consensus, without the phrase "he is trying to defy the odds".

Chapter Ten Faith & Fighting Spirit

In this chapter, I speak about my faith in Christ, my journey and obstacles I faced growing up, and ultimately how I battled and persevered to become the man I am today.

I was born in Paris and before I relocated to England, I loved life. My father would always tell me that education is the most important thing in a man's life, and that reading was important. He had studied Civil engineering in the Democratic Republic of Congo and he was a very smart man so for us his children my two siblings and I to get the best grades at school was vital. My mother supported him and made sure we attended school she always emphasized that one day we needed to become professionals. A tragedy happened when I was nine years of age my mother became severely ill and she was diagnosed with sarcoidosis a rare condition that usually affects the lungs, it causes shortness of breath and consistent cough. Because of this, she decided to relocate to the United Kingdom to join her younger sister who already lived here, as for my father he stayed in Paris.

My siblings did not really take to the United Kingdom and ended up going back to live with my father in France. Because I was really close to my mother and being her last born, I stayed here with her. At the age of nine, I started primary school and it was really hard to adapt especially the fact I could not speak English, I had this complex and I wanted to fit in. Before the first year of secondary school, I had learnt English and was able to

Interact, but I still felt like I was not able to fit in. Because of this, I was quiet throughout secondary school and there were other factors that contributed to me not engaging in my secondary school experience. The fact that I had seen my mother's health's deteriorate, that my family life had been destroyed at a very young age and also the fact that I missed living with my father. I was angry at the world, I was angry at life and I had yet to know why I had to go through so much as a young child. As a teenager, the hospital became my second home I had called the ambulance countless of times, ultimately that made me lose my faith. However, my mother, on the other hand, she kept talking to me about Jesus- Christ and that she would find her healing one day if we kept praying. Deep down inside of me something told me to believe but I also had doubts, because of how much I had seen my mother suffer and because of how my life had turned out. I never really engaged in school I never focused, I kept looking at my life circumstances and never envisioned things getting better.

This resulted in me leaving school with only one GCSE, and that only made matters worse because I started to think that I was an under-achiever, and ultimately, I did not believe in myself. At the age of sixteen, I came to the realisation that the only way to be noticed in my area was to be part of something that mattered. At the time, it seemed like joining a gang or being affiliated to one got you noticed. I also realised that it enabled individuals to fit in and that many that were not in gangs ended up becoming victims. So in my mind, I felt like adhering to a gang could be the answer to my troubles I felt like there were benefits that would come with this decision. Therefore, for a period I stuck by this decision I wore a mask and acted contrary to my upbringing done things in order to prove a point and be

Accepted. At the age of eighteen, I was still looking for my identity and I saw the respect that one could have if they had money. Therefore, I started to look in that direction of making money illegally I was very ignorant at the time and I felt like the world had not really been fair to me. So I embarked on the journey of making money illegally, after a while I had made some money and I wanted it to be shown. Therefore, I started to buy things that would show I had money. My ambitions were solely on acquiring material gain Cars, clothes and eventually a house.

One fateful day on the 1st January 2012, my life took a turn aged nineteen I attended a church service with no intention of giving my life to Jesus- Christ. A friend of mine to my surprise gave a testimony about the fact that he was supposed to go jail for a very long time, and that he had been acquitted of the crime. He was in tears and it was a very emotional day he also promised his mother that if he were to be found not guilty he would worship the God of his mother Jesus- Christ. That same day they gave an altar call and asked if anyone else had a testimony. I do not know what happened to me that day but I felt something strong in my spirit, that day I felt the Holy Spirit telling me to surrender. My body was shaking I do not even know how I ended up at the front but here I was with a microphone giving a testimony. I was very emotional I said how my life was in the past and how I believe Gods calling me today, it was like the story of Paul in Acts 9:3 it says that as he was approaching Damascus on this mission, a light from heaven suddenly shone around him. In the story, Paul fell off his horse when he saw the lord the same way I fell of my horse on the 1st of January 2012, the horse was the life of sin the life that I lived without Christ.

Two years later I was still a faithful servant, my life started to assemble, I developed a passion for reading the bible I aspired to become great and serve the lord just like I once did as a kid. When I was eight years, of age, I attended the consecration of one of my uncles who became a priest, and I remember standing up and shouting "this is how I want to be when I am older". Very bizarre how life can completely change can you imagine my first ambitions, as a kid was to become a pastor when I get older, but because of my life experiences and the influences that I had growing up in a particular area my life went the complete opposite. However, in all this, I am thankful because here I am now a servant of God he had everything under his control all the while.

Apart from all of this, the seed that my father had planted as a child started to come alive, so I went back to my education despite my insecurities. I had to start from an access to law course because I did not meet the requirements and then I was able to get into university. In all of this God was faithful and as we speak I am graduating in law in a few months. God changed my life; the man who once upon a time had low self-esteem became a community activist who works actively in his community trying to tackle crime, giving hope to the younger generation. Going into various schools where I grew up touching lives telling them my story, speaking to the kids who have low self-esteem and that do not have much confidence. Telling them that once an upon a time I was that kid and that if it's possible for me to now become a man of God, a role model in my community, a public speaker, a youth mentor, an aspiring law practitioner and now an author. It is possible for them to become who they aspire to be.

My name is Kevin Munga this is my story.

Acknowledgements

I would like to thank a few people.

Father: Mathias Munga   Uncle: Mira Mutombo

Mother: Scholastique Ngalula   Aunt: Mireille Feza

Keeley Stephenson - Spoken Word Artist and Youth mediator

Eamonn Madden - CEO of Inspirational Youth

Louise Hiller - Project Manager of Inspirational Youth

Ernest Kouassi -Young entrepreneur & author Hiba

Hussein - Law student Bridgette Ellis - Account

executive

Diego Hernandez - Law student

Ryan Hines - Disciple of Christ & Spoken Word

Artist Wesley Hines - Disciple of Christ & Educator

Gael Mukoko - Investment Banking recruitment

consultant Buba Otu – Disciple of Christ & Coach

Emmanuel Mensah – Disciple of Christ & Key Account

Manager Kenny Ventadour – Energy Engineering student

Orlane Bamanga - Marketing Graduate

O'Chain Gondorf – Duty Manager Execetera

Silas Mulumba – Entrepreneur

Joshua Bushell – Entrepreneur

Tyrone McFarlane – Business Student

About The Type

When writing the book "young black males have potential" I felt that many males coming from an ethnic minority were wrongly stereotyped and are ultimately looked down upon due to their race. I believe that by writing this informative book society will change its opinion of how they view young black boys, which will consequently bring about the change of opening many doors for these young men. I also think that this would be a positive incentive, as this will enable young black males to live their lives to their full potential ultimately leaving their mark on this planet, I wrote this book for a revolution to manifest and to highlight the fact that young black males do have potential.

Dr. Myles Munroe – "the greatest tragedy in life is not death, but a life without a purpose" [3]

---

[3] Myles Munroe. 2017. Quotable Quote. [ONLINE] Available at:
https://www.goodreads.com/quotes/309156-the-greatest-tragedy-in-life-is-not-death-but-a. [Accessed 28 September 2017].